The APARTMENT GUIDE

I0096769

TOM BRADLEY

THE APARTMENT GUIDE

THE APARTMENT GUIDE

TOM BRADLEY

SCRIPTOR HOUSE
THE EPITOME OF GREATNESS

Scriptor House LLC
2810 N Church St Wilmington,Delaware,19802
www.scriptorhouse.com
Phone: +1302-205-2043

© 2022 by Tom Bradley All rights reserved.
No part of this book may be reproduced, stored in a retrieval system,
or transmitted by any means without the written permission of the
author.
Published by Scriptor House LLC

Paperback ISBN: 979-8-88692-002-4
Ebook ISBN: 979-8-88692-003-1

Because of the dynamic nature of the Internet, any web addresses or
links contained in this book may have changed since publication and
may no longer be valid. The opinions expressed in this manuscript are
solely the opinions of the author and do not represent the opinions or
thoughts of the publisher and the publisher hereby disclaims any
responsibility for them. The author has represented and warranted full
ownership and/or legal right to publish all the materials in this book.

ABOUT THE AUTHOR

Over the years I have been living in different apartments. And I want to share with you what's involved in apartment life. So that you don't make the same mistakes that I made. Living in apartments cost money so you need to be careful about your decisions. I learned things the hard way and there was no one to give me advice. So, I am telling you the things that you will not hear from others. This book covers different topics that provide helpful information to help you make informed decisions. I enjoy the apartment life and these places can have all the conveniences needed right in the apartment complex. It is a community of neighbors that people live close together. And making friends while enjoying shared activities such as working out in the exercise room or hanging out in the club house. Also, it is nice to have the management there for you any time you when needed. So, I hope you enjoy this book and find it helpful.

CONTENTS

Chapter Four

Chapter Five

Chapter Six

Introduction

I want to start by saying thank you for your interest in this book. There is so much when it comes to apartment living. For most of my life I lived in apartments. And there are so, many pieces that come together when it comes to renting. From looking for that apartment that fits your needs. Weather it's a studio or a one bedroom. There is a lot to know from moving in and signing the lease along with everything else. Many of these apartment complexes are for active tenants. Offering amenities from an outdoor swimming pool and a club house that can provide activities such as a fitness area. So, there are things to do for those who want an active lifestyle. They also can offer wi-fi and their own laundry room. These places can just about offer everything you need with in the complex where you reside. Without having to drive everywhere. And all apartments are different from the price of the unit or offering less amenities. So, you can decide what apartment is best for you. Some apartments can offer promotions to attract a renter. In my book I break things down when it comes to different aspects when it comes to apartments. For over the years I learned from my mistakes and I wanted share with you. To help you make informed decisions which can make your move in a little more smoothly. And avoiding the big mistakes. Renting an apartment is very serious and with everything going on in life I think this book can help. The more you know then the better it is for you.

CHAPTER ONE

Finding your new apartment

I find the best way to find an apartment is by using the Apartmentguide. com and you can use this website www.apartmentguide.com/ apartments/New Jersey to go on their web site. And once you're on this website just put in your zip code and it will show you apartments in your area. Now it will give you pictures, prices and a phone number to call. They even show the location of the apartment complex on a map. The pictures are a virtual tour of the place and amenities that come with it. It's a good way to save time because these pictures show you what it's like and you will know what to expect. It also covers all counties in the state. So, if you're going to check out a few places then it could be helpful to bring a notepad and take some pictures what your smart phone. Write down any details about each place and include this with your pictures. And this will refresh your memory because there's a lot going on when you visit each place. It's also important to have all your documents in order and check your credit score. This way if you find something you like then you're ready, for apartments can go fast and you may miss the apartment that you wanted. I also suggest that you do an inspection and you can you use the inspection list from the book. And you can use this inspection guide to help you with the important things. Also, if you see something wrong talk to the management office and get it fixed before you move in. And if you see something in the place that concerns you such as for example a small hole in the wall. Then ask the office that if they do not correct it, then state it in the contract. Sometimes the landlord may feel that this problem is a little concern, but if it bothers you then it's best to include it in the contract. This way you will not be charged for it when you move out. This is a rare case for most apartments are in good condition. I also suggest taking the upper level as to taking the ground level. It may be little more money but it's less noise traffic from above. But if you want to save money the ground level is usually cheaper. Just always remember to keep windows locked when not at home.

About your lease

A lease is a contractual Arrangement between the the lessor and that would be the owner of the property and the lessee as the tenant. The lessee obtains the use of the property in return by paying regular rental payments. The lessee also agrees to abide by various conditions regarding the use of the property. I had enclosed an example of a lease that would be a legal document. Remember that not all leases are the same for each may have different terms and conditions. Also, it's important to understand the legal document because once it signed then it becomes binding. And in many cases if the conditions in this contract is broken such as example the rules of the apartment complex then it may result in fines or even worse conviction. Never signed a lease until you fully understand it. Also, it must be honored for the length of the agreement as stated in the terms of the lease. And keep in mind that if the lease is broken it can affect your credit score and the landlord could also seek civil judgment against you. And he can report you to a collection's agency. There is information from the state of New Jersey department of community affairs containing landlord and tenant information. It covers different topics that's informative to read. There is a small hand book that landlords should give new tenants but there's a chance the landlord may not have one. The title is called the Truth in Renting and it's a guide book on rights and responsibilities for residential tenants and landlords in New Jersey. I have also enclosed a cover page from New Jersey department of community affairs, so you can get this guidebook from the computer in the event the landlord does not give you one. This guidebook also covers some very important information for renters. The lease is the most important legal document that you will sign and knowing your rights is also very important.

TRUTH IN RENTING

A guide to the rights and responsibilities of residential tenants and landlords in New Jersey

New Jersey Department of
COMMUNITY AFFAIRS
101 South Broad Street,
PO Box 805
Trenton, NJ 08625-0805
www.nj.gov/dca

To view the complete DCA programs book, please visit
www.nj.gov/dca/publications

Community
AFFAIRS

Apartment renters have rights under the state of New Jersey. And the problem is that they do not know their rights. This is the front cover of a booklet called TRUTH in RENTING. And if you go online and type in Truth in Renting NJ.gov then you can download this booklet which covers a great deal of important information. Everything you need to know about your rights as an apartment renter which is about twenty-eight pages. And you print this booklet for your convenience.

Inspecting your new apartment

I would like to say that in many cases the condition of apartments is based on amount of rent. Also, what's included with the unit. When an apartment has low rent, you must inspect it thoroughly. There is a reason why it's so low so you need to be careful before you sign the lease. While for the most part many of the apartment complexes are in good shape. These places are a business and they know how to run it. Many have been in business for years. But there are others that fall behind. I like to deal with the big apartments as they can offer incentives to attract people looking to rent. And they can offer more amenities then the smaller apartment communities. Bigger businesses usually offer more than smaller ones. There are some apartment communities that are huge and they can have a lot to offer. I think that not only should you inspect the unit but find everything it has to offer. Walk the grounds and check out everything. Imagine that you are living there and see if you would like it. Also talk to people who live there and see what they think of the place. You can learn a lot by listening to people. And now you can get the big picture of everything it has to offer. Also, I like to write notes about every place that I have visited and compare them all together. Every apartment community has its own lifestyle with all its amenities such as a swimming pool and a club house. It's a matter of what you like and how much you are willing to pay. As you get into the big suburbs with its shopping districts and public transportation they can be expensive. The more there is to offer it seems the more it cost. The rent is the biggest part of the budget and you must be careful not to live above your means. These places have a legal contract and if it is broken you can be taken to court and evicted. So, everything must be right before you make the decision to sign the lease. Also, you should know about your tenants' rights that is coved in all municipalities. And it's important to read the contract. It covers everything in regards to legal binding between the apartment complex and the tenant. And one last point you need to find out about rent increases as in some places they can go up each year. And at some point, you may not be able to afford to stay there.

TENANT MOVE-IN AND MOVE-OUT PROPERTY CHECKLIST

Before you move-in and upon moving-out, be sure to carefully complete this check-list.

Tenant Name(s):

Address & Apt. No.:   City: State: Zip:

Move-In Date	Inspection Date:	Time:	By:
Move-Out Date	Inspection Date:	Time:	By:

Unless otherwise noted, the premises are in clean, good working order and undamaged. Use key below.

Key & Abbreviations:

NC: Needs Cleaning	**NSC: Needs Spot Cleaning**
NP: Needs Painting	**NSP: Needs Spot Painting**
NR: Needs Repair	**RP: Needs Replacing**
SC: Scratched	**Other:** _____

LIVING ROOM	Move-In	Move-Out	Cost
Floor			
Walls			
Ceiling			
Doors			
Windows			
Screens			
Shades			
Closet			
Elec Fix.			
Light bulbs			

KITCHEN	Move-In	Move-Out	Cost
Floor			
Walls			
Ceiling			
Doors			
Windows			
Screens			
Curtain			
Cabinets			
Drawers			
Sink			
Counters			
Fan/Light			
Elec Fix.			
Light bulbs			

REFRIGERATOR	Move-In	Move-Out	Cost
Inside/parts			
Outside			
Light			

STOVE/OVEN	Move-In	Move-Out	Cost
Outside			
Burners			
Vent			
Timer/Controls			
Surface			
Light			
Racks			
Drip pan			

DISHWASHER	Move-In	Move-Out	Cost
Inside/parts			
Outside			
Controls			

BATHROOM #1	Move-In	Move-Out	Cost
Floor			
Walls/Tile			
Ceiling			
Doors			
Cabinets			
Drawers			
Sink			
Shelves			
Mirror			
Tub/Shower			
Caulking			
Counter			
Fan			
Bowl/seat			
Towel rack			
Window			
Elec Fix.			
Light bulbs			

BATHROOM #2	Move-In	Move-Out	Cost
Floor			
Walls/Tile			
Ceiling			
Doors			
Cabinets			
Drawers			
Sink			
Shelves			
Mirror			
Tub/Shower			
Caulking			
Counter			
Fan			
Bowl/seat			
Towel rack			
Window			
Elec Fix.			
Light bulbs			

BEDROOM #1	Move-In	Move-Out	Cost
Floor			
Walls			
Ceiling			
Doors			
Windows			
Screens			
Closet			
Shades/Blinds			
Elec Fix.			
Light bulbs			

BEDROOM #2	Move-In	Move-Out	Cost
Floor			
Walls			
Ceiling			
Doors			
Windows			
Screens			
Closet			
Shades/Blinds			
Elec Fix.			
Light bulbs			

BEDROOM #3	Move-In	Move-Out	Cost
Floor			
Walls			
Ceiling			
Doors			
Windows			
Screens			
Closet			
Shades/Blinds			
Elec Fix.			
Light bulbs			

ENTRANCE/HALL	Move-In	Move-Out	Cost
Floor			
Walls			
Ceiling			
Doors			
Windows			
Screens			
Closet			
Shades/Blinds			
Elec Fix.			
Light bulbs			

DINING ROOM	Move-In	Move-Out	Cost
Floor			
Walls			
Ceiling			
Doors			
Windows			
Screens			

FRONT PORCH	Move-In	Move-Out	Cost
Elec Fix.			
Light bulbs			

BACK PORCH	Move-In	Move-Out	Cost
Elec Fix.			
Light bulbs			

GARAGE	Move-In	Move-Out	Cost
Floor			
Walls			
Ceiling			
Elec Fix.			
Light bulbs			

MECHANICAL	Move-In	Move-Out	Cost
Water Heater			
Smoke Det.			
Thermostat			
Furnace			
A/C			

# OF KEYS	Move-In	Move-Out	Cost
Front Door			
Mailbox			
other			

Comments: _____

_____

_____

_____

_____

_____

Move-In

Date _____ Signature _____ / _____ Move-Out Date _____

Date _____ Signature _____ / _____ Date _____

Date _____ Signature _____ / _____ Date _____

I/We (the tenant(s)) understand that unless otherwise noted, all discrepancies will be the tenant's tenant's responsibility and will be deducted from the security deposit at the time of move-out.

Move-In

Date: _____

Landlord/Agent Signature: _____

Move-Out

Date: _____

Landlord/Agent Signature: _____

Landlord and Tenant acknowledge that video and/or photos (digital or otherwise) have been taken of the premises. The original copies/files are in the possession of the ☐ Landlord / ☐ Tenant.

Tenant's Forwarding Address:

_____

_____

Apartment lease buyout

At least buyout is an option to break your lease in the event you must move out before the expiration date. I like the big apartment complexes because they usually provide this option. And this buyout cause can be found in the lease agreement. Sometimes things can come up and you must move out early before the lease ends, such as being transferred from your job to a new location. But breaking the lease is a penalty and it can be expensive. And the amount of the penalty can depend on how early you want to leave. It's best to go to the office management and discuss it with them and they can work you through the buyout procedure. The penalty can vary as in the earlier you leave the higher the penalty. But if you decide to take this option then it usually requires a letter. This letter is to terminate your apartment lease. Any office can help you to make this letter. But basically, you should indicate the day that you planned to break the lease and the reason you are leaving. And the address of your new residence. After its approved then you would submit a check for the penalty amount. And chances are they will do an inspection of the apartment before you move out. Now being that you left a forwarding address they will send your security deposit to your residence. So, it's best to clean and check your apartment and have it ready for this inspection. And it's best to keep all documentation that was made from the transactions pertaining to the buyout if needed.

Apartment Insurance

Apartment insurance is just another term for renters insurance. This type of policy helps ensure your personal belongings against natural disasters, thief and fire. Word of caution homeowner's policy's do not cover property damage from floods. And just to give you a basic idea, I will include a few important terms in this policy that you should know.

- Personal property coverage

Pays if the items in your condo unit such as furniture, clothing, computers and TV's are damaged, stolen or destroyed by a covered Loss.

- Loss of use coverage

Pays your additional living expenses {cost over the normal amount for housing, food, and other essential expenses} if you must temporarily move because of damage to your condo unit from a covered loss renders it uninhabitable.

- Medical payments coverage

Pays the medical bills of people hurt on your property. It might also pay for some injuries that happen away from the condo unit, such as your dog biting someone at the park.

These are just basic terms in a policy and when you are ready to purchase the policy, it's best to talk it over with the insurance agent.

What about the unexpected

Finding your apartment is a big step so you want to be careful that you don't make any mistakes. There are so many things that go along with having an apartment unit. And when you go over your budget you must add everything even including Public Storage. And it's important to have a savings to cover miscellaneous expenses such as doctor bills, dental and car repairs to say the least. It's good to have a cash flow of extra money at the end of each month to cover these unexpected expenses. You will have to expect rent increases just about every year. As some places have high utility bills such as gas heating. I suggest that it would be a good idea to find someone who lives in the building and ask that person about the rent increases any utility bills. Also, don't forget your apartment insurance policy. And remember that there's a good chance your rent will go up every year so you're going to need more money every time you renew your lease. So, I want to say it's important to plan long term for maybe a few years, in this apartment knowing that you can afford the rent increase every year. There always will be things that you did not planned for so it's very important to have a savings and have a cash flow to cover unexpected expenses. For in today's times anything can happen, and you always want to make sure that you have money to cover your living expenses. It's better to live within your means then having to struggle with the rent every month.

Problem with neighbor

When it comes to apartment rentals people come and go. And there is a possibility that someone can move in and things can change. For the most part people do get alone well together but at times they don't get along. Most of the time it's a noise issue. And living close together can make the problem worse. The one thing you don't want to do is get into an argument 'It's best to talk to management and have a private conversation about the problem. But if the issue gets worse there is another option that you can take and that is to talk to the management about moving into a different unit. This would be a last resort that you can take if you feel that you want to stay in the building. For sometimes it can be very irritating to have noise issues especially when you must go to work. So, if this is your option then you must talk to management right away because at times these apartments can go fast. And you can ask them to put you on the list for the next time an apartment comes available. This can give you peace of mind and avoid any conflicts with your neighbor. There are some big apartment complexes that have multiple buildings and you could even move into one of them. Some apartments have a lot of amenities to offer and it would be a shame to leave when all you must do is just relocate to another area. An apartment landlord will want to keep their good tenants so they will work with you.

When it comes to rent

For those who cannot afford higher rent there is another option and that is rent control rental apartments. Rent control refers to Laws or ordinances that set price controls on renting of residential housing. It functions as a price ceiling on residential rental property and a way of leveling everyone with affordable living. I enclosed three pages that relate to rent and Rent Control. I thought it would be best to give it to you from New Jersey Department of Community Affairs Division of Codes and Standards. And you can go on their web site if your looking for more information. This can give a little guidance when to comes to rent. I think one of the reasons people leave is the rent increases. It's a big part of your budget and it's important to understand about it. Try to find out as much as you can before moving in your new place. You can talk to a tenant that you see in the area and ask about it. Because it some places it can go up every year and force you to leave. And in the bulletins that I included where it when it comes to Rent Control it will give more understanding. It's important to search early for availability.

RENT INCREASE BULLETIN

New Jersey Department of Community Affairs
Division of Codes and Standards
Landlord-Tenant Information Service

RENT INCREASE BULLETIN

February 2008

This bulletin explains the process that a landlord must follow in order to increase a tenant's rent. This process may be based on rent control ordinances in specific municipalities; for rental units that are not governed by rent control ordinances the process is based on common law, which is set by common practice and case law. This bulletin is for informational purposes only and should not be used for legal interpretations or legal advice. Please consult an attorney for legal services and advice when necessary.

Applicability
The information in this bulletin applies to all residential rental properties including mobile homes, and land in a mobile home park. However, it does not apply to hotels and motels, and other guesthouses rented to transient or seasonal tenants.

Notice Required
Before the landlord can increase the rent he must provide the tenant with a written Notice to Quit and notice of the rent increase. (See Attachment A, Sample notice.) The Notice to Quit ends the existing tenancy. However, being served with a Notice to Quit does not require the tenant to vacate the rental premises.

The landlord must give notice within the timeframe stipulated within the lease (at least 30 days) or as stipulated within the local rent control ordinance, if any. If the tenancy is month-to-month the landlord must give a 30-day notice to Quit (given on the first day the rent is due).

Note: The Security deposit can be increased when the rent is increased but cannot exceed 1 ½ times the monthly rent.

When the Landlord May Increase the Rent
The landlord may only increase the rent at the beginning of the term of the lease. The landlord cannot increase the rent while a lease exists. The landlord must offer the tenant the option of entering into a new lease, at the increased rental rate, after the old lease expires. If the tenant does not sign the new lease and does not move at the expiration of the old lease and has been given a valid notice to quit and notice of rent increase, a new tenancy is automatically created at the increased rental rate.

2009 RENT CONTROL SURVEY

Refusal to Pay Rent Increase
If a tenant refuses to pay the rent increase and remains at the rental unit after the old lease expires (establishing new tenancy), the landlord may file a legal action in Superior Court to have the tenant evicted for failure to pay the rent increase. The landlord is not required to give the tenant notice before filing an eviction action for non-payment of the rent increase.

Unconscionable Rent Increase
If the tenant refuses to pay the rent because the tenant believes the rent increase is unconscionable or unreasonable, the tenant may withhold a portion of the rent. The tenant may withhold the difference between the old rent rate and the new increased rate. However, the landlord may take the tenant to court based on non-payment of rent increase, if this happens, the tenant may argue to the judge that the increase is unconscionable. The landlord has the burden of proving to the court that the rent increase is fair and not unconscionable.

Note: If the tenant chooses not to pay the rent Increase he should continue to pay the regular rent and be prepared to pay the full amount of the rent Increase if the court rules in the landlord's favor.

Determining if a Rent Increase is Unconscionable
In Fromet Properties Inc. v. Dolores Buel, et al., the court found that in determining unconscionability, the trial judge may consider: 1) the amount of the proposed rent increase; 2) the landlord's expenses and profitability; 3) how the existing and proposed rent compare to rents charged at similar rental properties in the geographic area; 4) the relative bargaining position of the parties; and 5) based on the judge's general knowledge, whether the rent increase would shock the conscience of a reasonable person.

Rent Control
The State of New Jersey does not have a law governing rent increases. However, municipalities within the State may adopt ordinances regulating the amount and frequency of rent increases within their specific municipality. A municipality's ordinance may not cover all rental units. To find out if a rent control ordinance exists, and if it applies to a specific rental unit, contact the municipal clerk in the municipality where the rental premises is located. (See Attachment B, Rent Control Survey.)

Exemption from Rent Control
Pursuant to N.J.S.A. 2A:42-84.2 through 2A:42-84.6, certain newly constructed multiple dwelling units may be exempt from rent control ordinances. Prior to entering into any lease for tenancy, the landlord of an exempt property must notify the prospective tenant that the rental unit is exempt from rent control. (See Attachment C, Newly Constructed Multiple Dwelling Law)

Public Financed and Subsidized Housing
Housing Developments owned or subsidized by the U.S. Department of Housing and Urban Development (HUD), the New Jersey Housing and Mortgage Finance Agency (HMFA) or regulated by the N.J. Public Housing and Development Authority are not subjected to municipal rent control ordinances. For proper procedures for notice and comments on rent increase for HUD buildings, call (973) 622-7900, ext. 3400 and (609) 278-7400 for HMFA buildings.

CHAPTER TWO

The dread of moving

It's good to keep a positive prospective when preparing to move. I And it seems the more you dread the thought then the harder it becomes. So, let's start by getting everything organized and I suggest the following:

Make a contact list of every one that handles your business matters such as your bank, credit cards, health insurance and so, worth.

- Contact the Postal Service and give them your new forwarding address.
- Contact the utility company when to turn off the electric at the old address and give the date to turn on the electric at your new place.
- Make sure you clean your old apartment including the appliances for chances are they will do an inspection before they clear you to leave.
- Give the Landlord your new address to send the security deposit.
- Mark all boxes with a marker such as Kitchen, Bathroom, etc.

This is a simple guide line to get you started and you may find other things to add on to it. So, take the time to make sure that you have everything covered, and things will go well.

Hiring a Moving Company

Moving can be expensive and stressful and finding the right moving company will require research. I find it better to hire a local moving company. For they had been in the business for years serving the community. But also, there are unscrupulous moving companies that are out there. So, you need to be careful when searching. I suggest you start your search on an internet website wwwmoving.org this is the American Storage Association. And they launched a consumer protection and certification program called Pro mover. It is designed to fight impostors known within the industry as rogue operators. Pro mover program helps consumers identify professional drivers. When on the website go to pro mover now and fill out your moving information. And you will receive quotes from licensed and insured movers. It's good to get a few quotes and compare. And you can also do a search on a mover by using the better business bureau. When you contact the moving company, chances are they will send forms. And in the forms would be an itemized list of what's going on the truck. They charge for the number of boxes that's going on the truck and the distance to your new place. It's important to have everything ready when they arrive. For if you make them wait there could be an extra charge. Also depending on the value of everything going on the truck, you will need to decide on the standard insurance or pay for an additional coverage.

I can do the moving by myself

When moving yourself there are things to consider. And I would like to start with choosing the moving truck. For a Studio and the One Bedroom Apartments you may get by with a 15ft truck. But it's best to consult with the truck rental company for their advice. I will give some basic advice as to items needed for loading the truck and purchasing the truck.

- Furniture Blankets to cover the furniture these are heavy blankets
- Hand truck for heavy items
- Load bar or tie downs to secure the furniture
- Plastic wrap for securing all items together
- Walk up ramp for loading depending on the vehicle height
- Insurance for the truck rental
- Make sure you know the vehicle height before driving under low bridges
- And you will pay for gas and millage
- And a credit card is needed to secure the purchase of the rental truck

And make sure that you have dependable people to help with the moving. Also, for this topic I am only referring to moving local and not out of state which is altogether different. It is important to load the truck properly which the heavy items should be in the center of the truck, for to much weight in the front or rear can cause handling problems when driving the truck. The other thing is making sure that the cargo is properly secured. For if the items get loose, they can get damage. When loading put the heavy boxes on the bottom and the lighter boxes on top and I like to use the heavy-duty plastic wrap to keep these boxes together. Even lose items that are not in boxes should be wrapped together with the plastic wrap. I would put any small items of value up front in the cab or put them in your car. And now as for the help there are a couple things to consider. First is to never hire people from the street to help with the moving. That is very dangerous, and you don't want these strangers to know where you live. The second part is the liability of someone who is helping and becoming injured during the move. And if the person who gets injured is family or a friend then that can be bad. That's why I prefer using a moving company. And they have the experience and the equipment to do the job right. Also, they have a big truck that can handle everything, and it takes the stress from you. So, you may save some money, but you take a risk when doing the move, yourself. The last thing and that's if a piece furniture become damaged by your friends unintentionally. For this can happen and if the moving company did the damage then you can report it for, they have limited insurance. And you can increase the moving insurance if your items have a high value.

Time to start packing

The most important part of your packing is to have the essentials ready right after you move into your new place. So, let's say it takes a couple days to get the important stuff put away. You want to be organized when you unpack your items. Imagine everything you need to set up each room with just the basic items you will need. And make a list for each room and let's say to hold you for a couple of days after you move into your new place. Now after you figured out the important items needed then you will place them on top of everything else in the box. This way when you open each box everything is there. And you do the same for each room. Also, in each list will be all the items in that box and leave the list on top of the items before you seal the it. So, when you open each box your list is on top of everything that's is in it and keep this list in the box until it is empty. Make sure you mark the front of each box with the name of the room. I suggest you use a permanent marker to label each box. And it's important to tell the moving men that when they stack the boxes to have the labels facing out so you can read them. This way all boxes have their label facing in one direction. One other thing that I think could be helpful is to buy plastic forks, knives and spoons and even have paper plates. Because it will take time to set up the kitchen. And these items can hold you over temporarily as you are setting up your cabinets in the kitchen and provide a easy meal.

When it comes to packing boxes

There are so many different types of moving boxes on the market today. And depending on your needs then I can say there are options. It's all about what's important to you for some people have expensive items so they will need special boxes. And I will explain about these boxes.

- There is the Flat screen tv carboard and shipping box. For those who may have expensive televisions and it can be used to ship a big mirror. Also, there are edge protectors that you can purchase that can be placed on each corner of the tv to provide a tight fit in the box.
- For those who have professional clothing there is a wardrobe box that has a rod through the top of the box. So, you can hang your clothes on the rod inside the box. Keeping your clothes clean and protected.
- Moving kits that come with an assortment of different boxes. And are purchased as a set of boxes.

I like the Bankers box for it's a heavy-duty box with a lid and it's good for protecting fine China and glassware. This box can have perforated dividers for your glasses. And I would add that you double the shipping packaging tape at the bottom of the box for a stronger protection. Also be careful not to put to much weight in the box for it puts extra stress on the box and the movers.

CHAPTER THREE

Apartment Security

Not everyone can afford to live in expensive luxury apartments. So, apartment security is very important for tenants. The more security devises the place has the better for you. And when you inspect the apartment unit you can ask what they have for security in and around the complex. Such as surveillance cameras, well lighted hallways and does the front doorway have an intercom for each unit in the building. I suggest that when you come to do an inspection of the apartment unit that you come on a Saturday. Some places will allow it and it's a good time to see how everything is like in the building when mostly everyone is off from work. For every apartment building has its own atmosphere. And after the inspection you can try to find a tenant talk in private and ask about the place. For the most part they are honest. If the person lived there for a while, then you can get a good idea of the place. And, I like to be taking a ride at night to check the place out. See if the complex has good lighting and are their people loitering around the building. And is the place quite in the evening when you want to relax. Some apartment complexes can have tenant meeting. And if your place does have these meetings then its good to get involved and voice your say in matters. For those who chose to live on the first floor, depending on the area you must always make sure you lock your windows before you leave the apartment. And it's good make sure your lease has a buyout option in case things get really bad.

Fire Safety

There is so much information out there on this subject. But I am doing to add things that you may not hear about. And I will be discussing fire safety for multi dwelling buildings. And I think tenants should have a plan when it comes to this kind of incident. Ask yourself what would I do in the event of a fire and do you know where the fire extinguishers located in the building? So, I will give my advice on things to think about. I will start by saying that if you must leave your apartment unit in a fire it's important to close your door to help contain the fire. And for those who live in the upper floors not to take the elevator, for in the event the power goes out in the building that you can be trapped inside it. So, I think it best to take the stairwell instead. If there are disable tenants on your floor, make sure to tell the fire fighters so they can assist in getting them out. Also, for those disable tenants who have wheelchairs that live on the upper floors, then I suggest that you speak to the management to put you on the first level of the building for your safety. Always remember that door handles can be hot when touching from the heat in the area. And one of the most important things you can do is to keep all your important documents together so in an emergency you can grab then and this will save time leaving the building. Make sure you have your apartment insurance documents with your other papers that you will take when leaving the building. And put the insurance phone number in your smart phone. It's always good to have an emergency savings in the event something happens. Money that is available in an emergency such as a fire. So, you need to go through all your important documents and figure out what to take with you in an emergency. Just try to throw then in a carrier bag or shopping bag in a fast matter. And make sure you call the apartment insurance company right away to get started on your claim. Having this insurance is the most important documents you can have at this time. And having an emergency savings will hold you over for when the insurance money comes. Remember this insurance covers your belongings to help you to start again. Along with other important information about your coverage. Also, if you must relocate to another place make sure you leave a forwarding address with the U S Postal Service. I just say this to remind you because it is very important. The one thing about apartment living is that much of our belongings is in the apartment unit. And that is a big lost to a tenant. Although some people may have some of there belongings in public storage, they may fair a little better but it's still a big lost. Fire safety is every one's responsibility and if you see what may appear to be a fire hazard then report it. Do not expect others to do it for it may not get reported.

Surveillance stickers for apartment

In life we can't take things for granted and that goes for protecting your property. And some apartment buildings have a high turn over with people moving in and out. And this creates a problem that you cannot always depend on your neighbors. With older apartment buildings some how strangers can always find a way to get in the building. So, for those who can't afford a home surveillance system. There is another option and that is to put fake surveillance stickers on your window or door that reads 24 hr. surveillance. And if you are not allowed to put one on your door then put it somewhere it can be seen when someone enters the apartment. A thief may not want to enter this apartment if he thinks there is a video camera watching. The idea to fake out someone in thinking they are on camera. They can be purchased from Amazon and they look real. But of course, there is a chance that these stickers may not work. Another suggestion also would be to put up a large sign for anyone coming in to see that says Smile Your on Camera. And that will make anyone think twice. Do not tell anyone that your surveillance system is fake for you don't want word to get out. But I must stress that having apartment insurance is critical in the event your apartment is broken in to and at least your insurance will reimburse for you for your possessions. This way if the fake stickers don't work at lease you will not lose out altogether.

Surveillance Camera

Today home security has become a lot more affordable. And even if you rent a small apartment unit it's inexpensive to install a surveillance camera. So, I am going to talk about installing one and if you have a smart phone and wi-fi in your apartment then you can install it. There are many different types on the market. And I start by talking about only one just to give you a basic idea of this camera. I have the ezviz mini o home monitoring security camera and it sells for around thirty-five dollars. It gives a good view of the room in HD and it also has night vision. Even when the room is dark you can see the room clearly. So, you would install the ezviz app on your smart phone and it will link with your wi-fi and camera. After it's installed you can see the room and when you don't want the camera on just go on the app and give it a small tap to put the camera to sleep. Then when you are ready again to turn it on just go to the app and give it a small tap to wake it up. So, when using this camera everything is done through the app. It also has motion detection alerts and you can install a SD Card to store up to 128 gb of storage. I like this camera for its affordability and the options that come with it. But I am only using this camera as an example for their many others on the market. It's comforting to know that when you are away from home that at any given time, you can see your apartment room on your smart phone. As apartment renters the apartment can hold most of all your possessions.

Spy Cameras

Spy cameras are very popular today and they are good to have in the apartment. And you have so much in your apartment unit it's nice to keep an eye on things. If someone is in your place the person would feel uncomfortable seeing a camera in the room. But the hidden camera cannot be seemed. If you are busy at work and you cannot find the time to stay home as maintenance comes to do repairs. Then it's good to have this hidden camera on as they are working. And if you are a senior and have a cleaning person in your place this camera will also come in handy especially when the person is cleaning rooms. There are so many different types of cameras on the market. And I like to think that it should be something that has a functionality for your use, while also serving as a camera. So, let's say you need to buy a clock radio for the bedroom and instead of getting a regular radio, why not get a clock radio with a hidden camera in it. And in this way, it will serve a dual purpose. Here are a few different ideas as for hidden cameras for your rooms, but there are a lot more to consider.

- TV sound bar with hidden camera for the living room
- Tower fan that's a real fan and hidden camera
- Blue tooth speakers with a hidden camera

CHAPTER FOUR

Apartment Furniture

Most apartments require smaller furniture because of the small rooms. And the worst thing you can do is buy the wrong furnishings for your apartment unit. You need to research, and this takes a little time. My suggestion is to take measurements of the area where this furniture piece will go. And you can take out your smart phone or camera and take a picture of that area. When taking the picture do a wide view. Now when you look around you will bring the measurements and the picture with you. Now as you are looking for that furniture piece you will have a good idea of how this new furniture piece will blend in the room from your picture. And when buying small furniture, you can avoid clutter by buying small. Such as for example accent stands, love seat sofa for the living room these are good for space saving. And the smaller the apartment unit the more space saving you will need. There are so many clever ideas on the market that are excellent for space saving furniture. So, if you type in the computer space saving furniture this could be a good place to start. Now you can get an idea of what's out there and look for furniture that is functional such as for example accent stands with built in shelves and while I am on the this subject of accent stands you can put a table lamp on top and have the shelves for storage. I would do this then to buy a floor lamp which has no functionality and is a waste of space.

Department store furniture

It seems at one time the big department stores would have a large furniture section. But today they are getting harder to find. For the most part much of the furniture comes from their online service. And it makes it harder when you cannot see the furniture at the store. So, you must be certain that this what you want before the purchase. And when it comes to apartment store furniture things get more complicated. They offer a lot for home furnishings, but you may not have a good selection when it comes to smaller furniture. So, you need to check all your sources as to what store can offer what you need. There is an upside to buying from these stores. And if you have a store credit card then they can offer some pretty good deals. If you can hold out for the big holiday sales, then they can offer good discounts. Also, you can apply your reward points along with long term financing and with free shipping. And as a value customer you are treated better if in the event there is a problem with the furniture. For they want their loyal customers to be happy. But here again you may not find a good selection for the piece of furniture that you want. But if you are not fussy then this could be a good option. There is a very important part of the delivery service that I must mention. And that is to inspect the furniture when delivered as the delivery men are present. So, they can witness if there is damage and ask them to notate it on the invoice for your damage claim.

Shopping furniture stores

For some reason furniture stores come and go just like so, many other stores. So, you need to be careful where you shop. But I still believe there are a lot of good stores. I like coming in the store and you can see everything in person. Although there is limited selection you can still find what you like or something close. There are so, many different furniture stores and they come big and small. And at times the salesmen can be knowledgeable having years of experience. And you don't always have to go to the big stores to find a good deal. For every store is different when it comes to their furniture. Not to mention they offer discounts sales and long-term financing. And there are stores that can have unique furniture that stand apart from the other stores. For they can offer a wide variety of furniture that makes it fun to shop. So, take a ride and check these stores out just to see what's out there. You can take a picture with your smart phone of the area in the room where your new furniture will go. And write the measurements along with the picture. Now you can get an idea how the new furniture will blend with the room. And furniture salesmen can help with this kind of stuff. It's always nice to get a second opinion with someone who knows the business. Also, they usually have furniture online on their web sites and this can offer more selection for what you need. For example, a piece of furniture that you like that can come in different colors.

Furniture shopping online

The best source for apartment furniture is searching online. This way you can see the on-site pictures. Along with all the detailed information. And there you can see an assortment of other furniture that is in the category to what your searching. And one piece of furniture can be showed in different colors of wood or fabric and including the measurements. So, it gives a good idea of what's out there. A lot better then going to a store that will limit options such as selection of colors or other features that you will get online. The downside to online shopping is the fact that you can not see this furniture in person. If you are a little worried about buying the big items online then you can buy those big items in the store and buy the smaller items online. After all they will need to assemble when deliver to your apartment. Remember one thing when you're ready to purchase it's important to get it right the first time. And if you buy the wrong furniture, you're going to have to look at it every day. Good furniture will last for years and that's nice to see every day. It will highlight the appearance of the room. And done right the small pieces of furniture will stand out and not look cluttered in a small room. There are so, many web sites that do well in selling this furniture. It is important that you make sure you have your measurements correct before the purchase. And to check out as many places of furniture as you can because they offer different types and styles.

Restoring used furniture

One way to save money is to shop around for used furniture. And there are a lot of places to look such as yard sales, flea markets and even stores. But these places usually have a no refund or return policy. So, it's very important to make sure you can restore this piece of furniture and give it a close inspection. And if the furniture has been in humid conditions then there is a chance of wood warpage. And sometimes a piece of furniture may look like junk but if examined close you may see that it can be restored. Sometimes people want to get rid of their furniture. And they may have a yard sale or post an ad in the newspaper. But these sales can be negotiated on price and you may get a good deal. So, let's say that you are interested in restoring used furniture. Well there are options that you have such as furniture stores can have damage furniture that they want to get rid of for a low price and you can fix yourself. Also, there are home improvement stores that supply a lot of things needed to do the restoring of used furniture. You can even go on U tube and watch video clips of people showing how to do basic furniture restoring. And for instance, if a sofa or chair has a tear in it and is in good condition you can also throw a furniture slipcover over it. So, you will need to buy the materials and invest time to do the project. But the result is that you can restore this piece of furniture any way you like. Such as what color to paint it or change the fabric. And save money in the process.

CHAPTER FIVE

Improving the kitchen

It seems apartment kitchens are never big enough. And storage is always an issue. So I like to think as the kitchen and the dining room as one. For they both work well together when storing all the kitchen necessities. And now I will give suggestions to help improve the kitchen.

- Kitchen counter top
- Upper kitchen cabinet
- Lower kitchen cabinet
- Using the kitchen cart

One problem with the kitchen counter top it can have to much clutter. It's best to use small appliances to save space. And there are a lot of counter top organizers to help improve space. And for the upper kitchen cabinets you can use shelf organizers. For the lower kitchen cabinets you can use organizers for storage. And use the bottom oven drawer for added storage. As for the drawers I like the expandable drawer dividers. These expandable dividers will stop the drawer clutter. And for the kitchen sink area you can install a under sink two tier organizer. This organizer is design to fit around the plumbing pipes. And last I like the kitchen cart. And it can be used in different ways. One is the use of the counter top along with the storage space below. They also come with wheels so you roll it out of the corner and when done roll it back and it can be use as serving cart.

Improving the dining room

The dining room can serve as two functions as a dining area. And it also serves as additional storage for the kitchen. Being that the kitchen has limited storage space. So, I think that putting in the right furniture that this room can provide this function. Depending on the size of the room will determine what kind of furniture will fit. And now I will give suggestions that can help improve this room.

- Pub dining set
- Drop leaf dining table set
- Kitchen dining room cart
- Tall pantry cabinet
- Dining room buffet cabinet

As for a small dining area or a studio apartment I think the pub dining set will do well. They can come as a small space saving dining set. And the drop leaf dining table set is also good for this table can be adjusted. So, this table can be use for different size rooms. The kitchen dining cart is nice for it can provide a small countertop and has shelfs for storage. It also has wheels so it can be moved anywhere as needed. And the tall pantry cabinet does not take up wall space. You can put it in the corner, and it can hold a good amount of storage. And last is the dining room buffet cabinet which is good for a larger room and does well for storage and it is also attractive for the room.

Improving the living room

I want to start by saying having so stuff in an apartment unit can be a challenge. And trying to keep the room from clutter can be done if you organize your furniture furnishings. By putting in multi-use furniture. The more multi-use furnishings will help create more functionality by having one-piece furniture serve more than one purpose. And having a nice room that can hold more storage without clutter. It is hard to give a mane for furniture because one-piece of furniture can have different names. So, I will describe furniture that you can look up online to get an idea of what I am talking about. These furniture pieces that I am listing can help improve the room.

- Ladder shelf
- Organizer cube bookcase
- Loveseat sofa
- Small end table with cabinet door
- Storage tower

You can go on Amazon and see what they are and get an idea if one of these can help improve your living room. And I also picked these out for a reason. If renting the landlord does not allow nails or screws in the wall. So, everything needs to be supported by it's self and not mounted to the wall. And to save on wall space its best to put in anything that extends the shelfs vertically. Such as the Ladder shelf for example.

Improving the bedroom

I want to talk about making the room a little more functional. And if you have a small bedroom then this can be a challenge. So, I will start by saying there are three main parts of the room when it comes to storage. And in my opinion that would be the dresser, bed and closet. Remember I am only referring to a small bedroom. And I will go lightly with helpful suggestions. I want to start with the dresser. I think for example using a five-drawer chest next to a dresser is a good way to save space along the wall. This chest will do well if you have a low ceiling in the room. It has drawers above each other and does not take up much wall space. Allowing space for a normal size dresser which when used both together will save on wall space and hold more of your belongings. But its best to measure the furniture first to see how they will fit together. If the chest is to high with a low ceiling it will look to big for the room. Its best to find furniture that will fit your needs for the room. And keep in mind that you want this furniture to be able to fit in another bedroom in the event you may have move to a different place. The idea would be that this furniture would fit in any apartment. For all apartments has different size rooms. And now the bed which can be used for storage. You can purchase under bed storage containers. They come clear so you can see through and they can come with wheels on the bottom making it easy to roll out. For the closet if you rent do not customize it.

Improving the bathroom

The bathroom is different from the other rooms because of the humidity. And this room needs to have furnishings that can take the humidity from the shower. Depending on the humidity in the bathroom, the one thing to be careful is having your furnishings made of wood. Because over a period the humidity could cause wood warpage. And I am saying that there is a chance. So, there is another option and that is to use furniture furnishings made of metal construction and rust resistant. This option is good if you don't want to take a chance on regular wood furniture. And if you want a better quality of wood furniture, then I suggest Teak wood and Bamboo furniture which will do well in humidity. And now I will give suggestions that I think can help this room.

- Expandable under sink organizer and storage
- Tall cabinet linen tower
- Etagere over the toilet storage
- Slim bathroom floor cabinet

I think these items can help improve the bathroom and they are space saving. But this is only part of what is out there on the market. Bathrooms come in all sizes and you can do well if the room is big enough. But if you have a small bathroom then you need to check out all your options that is space saving. I tried to explain these items so you can research them online.

CHAPTER SIX

Thinking about public storage

For apartment living storage is a big issue. It's hard enough to find storage for every day needs in your apartment unit. And over time we just have to much stuff. I am very cautious about public storage. It can be expensive if you do the long-term storage. They offer promotions and discounts to attract your attention. Such as for example free rent for the first month or a discount on the first two months rent. Enticing you to purchase a long-term lease agreement. So, if you are ready then I can give suggestions to help get you started. When you come to check out the place see if they offer a good surveillance of the facility. And look for a gated entrance access along with good lighting of the grounds and inside the place if it's a building. For there will be times you come at night. And I prefer an onsite manager on the premises if needed. Some storage facilities may require you to purchase storage insurance which they would usually sell. But not all require insurance so you will need to ask. But having insurance on your storage will give you piece of mind. And depending on the value of your storage you may need it, for at times these places can be busy and anything can happen. I also think that if you decide to rent then consider an automatic payment system. Which the management will help set up for you. Being these are recurring payments this will prevent late fees. And non-payments can result in default and having you locked out of your storage. So, it is important to pay on time.

Indoor storage units

There comes a time when we just have to much stuff. Weather it's making extra room for your sports items or just running out of space in the apartment. There will come a time when you must ask do, I really need all this stuff? Because at this point it will cost you money for self-storage. And the larger the unit space then the more money it will cost and let's not forget adding storage insurance. So, the nice part of these indoor storage units is that everything is inside protected from the weather. And this building can come as non-climate control, or it can have climate control. Now a little about climate control is it regulates the indoor temperature of the building. Which will help protect your items. And usually they offer a unit size guild to help you determine how much storage space you may need. And I will give you basic unit sizes that a you can find in self-storage just to show you what's out there.

- Small self- storage unit 5'x5'
- Small self-storage unit 5'x10'
- Medium self-storage unit 5'x15'
- Medium self-storage unit 10'x10'

I will stop here because these would be average for apartment tenants. And the large storage units are very big and would not be practical for apartment use. Also, these places are well managed in getting you set up.

www.ingramcontent.com/pod-product-compliance
Lightning Source LLC
Chambersburg PA
CBHW060255030426
42335CB00014B/1708

* 9 7 9 8 8 8 6 9 2 0 0 2 4 *